World of Bugs
BEASTLY BEETLES

By Greg Roza

Gareth Stevens
Publishing

Please visit our Web site, www.garethstevens.com. For a free color catalog of all our high-quality books, call toll free 1-800-542-2595 or fax 1-877-542-2596.

Library of Congress Cataloging-in-Publication Data

Roza, Greg.
  Beastly beetles / Greg Roza.
     p. cm. — (World of bugs)
  ISBN 978-1-4339-4600-4 (pbk.)
  ISBN 978-1-4339-4601-1 (6-pack)
  ISBN 978-1-4339-4599-1 (library binding)
  1. Beetles—Juvenile literature. I. Title.
  QL576.2.R69 2011
  595.76—dc22
                                        2010034392

First Edition

Published in 2011 by
Gareth Stevens Publishing
111 East 14th Street, Suite 349
New York, NY 10003

Editor: Greg Roza
Designer: Christopher Logan

Photo credits: Cover, pp. 3, 5 (all), 7, 9, 11, 17, 19, 21, 24 (all) Shutterstock.com; p. 1 Ablestock.com/Thinkstock; p. 13 Jupiterimages/Photos.com/Thinkstock; p. 15 John Foxx/Stockbyte/Thinkstock; p. 23 Baerbel Schmidt/Digital Vision/Thinkstock.

Printed in the United States of America

CPSIA compliance information: Batch #CR118221GS: For further information contact Gareth Stevens, New York, New York at 1-800-542-2595.

BEASTLY
BEETLES

One out of every four animals is a beetle!

A beetle has six legs.

7

A beetle has two feelers.

9

A beetle has four wings.

Two wings are hard.

13

Two wings are for flying.

14

15

Most beetles eat plants.

17

Baby beetles look like worms.

19

The diving beetle can swim.

Some beetles are big!

Words to Know

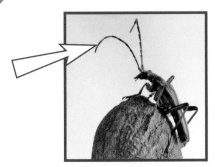

feeler

leg

plant

wing

24